Robert W. James

C++ for Beginners

First steps of C ++ programming language

Table of Contents

C++ for Beginners
Simplified Guidebook for People with Zero Programming Experience
Introduction
Chapter 1: Let's Get Started

Algorithms
Compilers and Programming "Languages"
 Integrated Development Environment
Chapter 2: Your First C++ Program

Hello World Initiatory C++ Program
Install an Integrated Development Environment for C++
Now Back to the Source Code
Comments in C++
Multiple Line Screen Output

Chapter 3: Let's Do Some Math

What is a Variable?
Get Creative with Your Identifiers
Reserved Words
Allowed Characters
Variables vs. Constants
Punctuators

Chapter 4: Let's Do More than Just Math

Types of Operators
Conditional Operator
Operator Precedence
Programming Exercise

Chapter 5: Data Types

Fundamental Data Types

String Class
Variable Initialization
Type Conversions

Chapter 6: Input and Output

Chapter 7: Conditional Statements in C++

Conditional Statements

Chapter 8: Loops

For Loop
While Loop
Do While Loop
Jump Statements
Go to Statement
Break Statement
Programming Exercise
Continue Statement

Chapter 9: C++ Functions

What is a Function?
Function Declarations
Built-In Functions

Chapter 10: Arrays

What is an Array?
Array Declaration
Multidimensional Arrays
Programming Exercise
Accessing Multi-Dimensional Array Elements
Programming Challenge
Answer to Programming Challenge

Chapter 11: Pointers

What is a Pointer?

Declaring a Pointer
Making Use of Pointers
Moving Forward
What is OOP?
Classes vs. Objects
A Final Word

Introduction

Thank you for downloading this book "C++ for Beginners: A Practical Guidebook for Anyone without Any Programming Experience."

The premise of this book is already laid out on the title. I assume that you, the reader, have no prior experience whatsoever to any kind of computer programming. What this book does is that it teaches you the principles behind programming and encoding.

Sure, we will go over the "how" and the "what" of programming. But to help you further understand how a computer program is built you need to understand the why behind it all.

And that is why we will go over the absolute basics.

Along the way you will learn a lot of technical jargon. Yes, every industry from farming to robotics has its own set of weird technical language that only the people who delve in such things understand.

Here's a bit of hard cold truth: the same is true when it comes to C++ programming (or programming in general). You have to learn the jargon. You need to eventually understand what each of the programming words and terms mean. In short, you need to learn to talk the talk of programming.

This book will go over that. But don't worry — we will only go over the beginner's jargon. In fact, we will only cover enough jargon so you can make a functional C++ program. We will also explain each term well enough in layman's terms so that you can understand and explain them to someone else who is also not so programming savvy.

I have included a lot of programming examples on this book as well as exercises to help you understand how each snippet of code works. As you go along through the lessons you will be showed how each part of the code fits together. I try not to be operating specific when I write the examples in this book. So it doesn't really matter that much if you are using Linux, Mac, or Windows. But just so you know when I wrote the sample codes that you see here I was using Windows 10. But the code itself is not native to a certain OS.
In this book we will go over the fundamental language features of C++ as well as all its standard library components (okay that's a jargon right there—well, I'll explain what that is in one of the chapters of this book).
We will go over the rationale behind the code as well. I will describe possible problems that each line of code will help to solve. We will also go over the underlying principles of certain parts of a C++ program, which of course includes possible limitations it may have.
Remember that C++ as a programming language has changed and developed through the years. Today it is a lot easier to use than what it was before yet it remains true to the lofty goals of its predecessor's, the C programming language.
Now, finally, you may have heard that C++ is a programming language that has that reputation of being not easy to learn. Yet, however, it remains as the language preferred by professional programmers.
And that is why I am trying to convey the language to you in the simplest way ever, so that we can get over that initial impression. Once you get past that, you will see that C++ is quite enjoyable. When that happens, you will find the rest of the steps into advanced C++ programming to be quite easy.

It all starts with a thorough understanding of the basics, which is what we will cover in this work.
Thanks again for downloading this book.

Chapter 1: Let's Get Started

C++ is one of the many programming languages highly used today. A computer program is logical set of logically arranged instructions that you give to a computer that it can perform in order to accomplish or complete a certain task.

Algorithms

This logically arranged set of instructions is called an algorithm. Think of it as a recipe. The instructions in an algorithm need to be performed sequentially or else you won't get the desired result.
For instance, let's say theoretically that you are programming a computer to bake a cake. You can't start with adding the icing, followed by mixing the batter, and finally heating the oven to 400 degrees while everything is inside. That's just not going to work. Just remember that you should organize the instructions that you will program in a logical manner.

Compilers and Programming "Languages"

Computers don't have a language just like what we humans use or refer to as a language. A computer doesn't talk per se but it can communicate — well just not in English or some other human language. They communicate using electrical signals usually via a series of on and off signals. They use a series of ones and zeroes to communicate with other pieces of electronics.

This is called machine language. Now, this is a very simple explanation of what machine language is. In reality it is a bit more complex than that. Just remember at this point that computers communicate that using that kind of code.

As you will see later on, C++ is a high level language. That simply means it resembles human speech. A lot of the commands that you will be using to write and compose your algorithms (i.e. your logical series of instructions) will somewhat look like English — in fact you will use a lot of English words in the process.

A high level programming language is one that you can read and decipher so you can ascertain its meaning. Just by going through the code you will be able to at least get an idea what certain parts of a C++ program is doing.

Now, here's the thing. Computers don't understand high level languages. Even though C++ and other programming languages are already pieces of code, computers still won't be able to understand them.

That means you will need a translator.

You still need to translate all your C++ programming code into machine language. The good news is that there are translator programs that were designed to grab your almost English C++ code into that binary code (i.e. the series of ones and zeroes that was mentioned earlier) so that a computer can understand your instructions.

Your C++ program is also referred to as the source code. The compiler's job is to go through your source code from beginning to end and translate it into machine readable code one line at a time.

Once it is translated then the computer can understand the instructions that you included in your program. However, there is one more step that needs to happen before your computer program can be executed. Remember that all of this happens at lightning speed. This is the process that happens every time you tap a button or swipe on your phone's screen. It also happens when you click something or even when you type on your computer keyboard.

The machine readable code that the compiler produces is called an object file. As stated earlier, there is still one more step necessary in order to turn your computer into a program that your computer can use.

Your object file will be passed on to another program called a linker (it is also called a binder). What this other program does is that it links or binds certain commands from an entire library of commands already included in C++ that a computer can understand. A lot of these are important computer functions and processes that work in the background that you won't have to worry about for now.

Integrated Development Environment

Now, you don't have to think about how your source code (i.e. the computer program) that you will write gets translated to machine readable instructions. However, in order to get all of that done you will need to install an app or computer software that is known an IDE or Integrated Development Environment.

An IDE is an app that does all of the processes described above so that you can focus on writing your C++ program. It's like a word processor but with extra programming related functions.

You will get an area where you can type and edit your C++ code. Once you're done the IDE will go over your source code using a compiler to translate your code. During this process the IDE will also check your source code looking for possible errors.

If anything as much as a misspelled command (or any other error) is found, then the IDE will stop compiling and it will report the error to you. You can then make the necessary corrections and restart the compiling process all over again.

Note that an IDE is actually a full suite of different applications and programs all packaged into one. It includes at least the following:

- *Text Editor* – this is the program or app that you use to write and save your source code.
- *Compiler* – this is the app that you use to translate your source code from human readable code to its machine (aka computer) readable version.
- *Debugger* – this is the app that evaluates your code, i.e. it's the app that checks your code for errors (aka bugs — don't ask me, that's what they called them)

There are other apps and tools in an IDE that are pretty useful to make sure that the computer program or app that you are writing will be launch ready with no errors or bugs. You don't just write several lines of code and think you're done. In the program development process you will be doing a lot of product testing.

You will fine tune, correct errors, and tweak sections of a program until all the bugs have been worked out. Well, at least now you know what the majority of the work you'll be doing eventually.

Chapter 2: Your First C++ Program

Now, this is some sort of a tradition – consider it as your rite of passage into the world of C++ programming or programming in any kind of language to be exact. I typed the short source code below to illustrate what a C++ program looks like when you compose one.

Hello World Initiatory C++ Program

This one is a rather simple program. All it does is display "Hello World!" on the screen. A lot of programming tutorials start with that so I guess you should start with that as well. At least you will get a brush of what it is you're going to be doing eventually.

Now, here's the sample source code:

```
#include <iostream>
using namespace std;
int main()
{
cout << "Hello World!";
return 0;
}
```

As you can see I didn't use an IDE to write that code. I just used Notepad++ (it's a text editor) which also works if all you want to do is write your code and nothing more. Now, before going over that source code and the different basic elements of a C++ program, I would like you to download an actual IDE and install it on your computer.

Install an Integrated Development Environment for C++

Find one that works on the operating system that you are using. I recommend the following IDEs in case you don't know which ones to look for. Here are my top 5 integrated development environments for C++ programming:

1. *Eclipse*: this is a popular integrated development environment for both C and C++ programming languages. What I like about this IDE is that it is very easy to use — there are no complicated menus and everything is pretty straightforward. Here are some of the key takeaways for Eclipse:
- It is open source, which means it is free.
- It supports different operating systems such as Mac OS X, Linux, and Windows.
- It has a refactoring feature — this means you can restructure parts of the code during the editing process without directly affecting external behavior. This is a useful function to test changes that you want to make in a C++ program before actually making them.
- Other features include auto complete feature, profiling, compiling, and debugging.
- It provides code analysis
- Drag and drop features

2.   *GNAT Programming Studio*: GNAT Programming Studio, or GPS for short, is another free IDE but this one is a lot more advanced compared to Eclipse. If you have some programming experience then you can get this one. I would say that if you are an absolute beginner at programming in general you can start with other IDEs and then move to GPS after you have become familiar with development environments and their features.

Here are the key takeaways for GPS:
• Supports multiple platforms (aka different operating systems)
• It is free to use
• Browser like design
• Also uses code refactoring
• Includes lots of drag and drop features. That means the user interface is highly customizable — work with all the tools that you usually use.
• The package includes the following features: auto complete feature, profiling, code coverage, debugging, compiling, and a whole lot more.

3.   *Netbeans C++ IDE*: this is another advanced IDE but I guess it is a bit simpler compared to GPS. So, maybe if you are kind of tech savvy let's say you've been tinkering around a bit with Photoshop menus and other graphical user interfaces that are a bit more complex than your run off the mill app, then maybe (just maybe) you can get the hang of using Netbeans.

Oh yes, as a bit of a fair warning, Netbeans will contain a lot of templates that are usually project based. It may take a toll on your computer if you are using an older system.

Here are the key takeaways for this IDE:
- It is open source, which means it is absolutely free.
- It supports refactoring and it also features code completion
- This is a cross platform IDE.
- It comes with a gdb debugger which is a more powerful debugger
- Its features include the following: lots of templates, bracket matching, code folding, a variety of formatting styles (organizes your code which makes it a lot more readable), semantic highlighting, and automatic indentation.
- Supports both C and C++
- You can use this IDE and its tool on a remote host. That means you can connect to a client system and debug and edit the programs and source code stored there.

4. **CodeLite**: this is another free cross platform integrated development environment for C and C++. If you don't like the complicated menus and other options in GPS and Netbeans then this one might be a good fit for you.

Here are some of the key takeaways for this IDE:
- Uses a next generation debugger
- Errors are clickable through the build tab
- Provides generic support for other compilers
- Features include profiling, class browser, refactoring, and static code analysis
- Also features the RAD tool, which can be used for building applications that are widgets based.

• It comes with a powerful and fast code completion tool.

5. *Visual Studio Code*: if you are looking for a highly customizable cross platform advanced IDE then this could be a good option. This integrated development environment was developed by Microsoft and you wouldn't believe it if I told you — this one is actually free.

Most of the time you would think that if this is a Microsoft product then you have to pay for it. That's how it usually is, right? But not this one — this is one of the few products that are on their list that isn't on sale.
Now, on top of that, this IDE is cross platform, which means that it also runs on Linux and Mac OS. Because of that and a lot of marketing, this IDE also has a lot of users, which means that you can find a lot of support online in case you get stuck somewhere.

Here are its key takeaways:
• It features snippets, code refactoring, and intelligent code completion
• It has a rich API that you can use for debugging your source code
• Even though it has a simple graphical user interface, VSC has integrated GIT
• If you prefer to do things via command line then this IDE comes with a command line interface

Now Back to the Source Code

As stated earlier, you should install an IDE first and then enter the above mentioned sample C++ code. If you run that (see the instructions for the IDE of your choice on how to run the code that you typed) you will see the following displayed on your screen:
Hello World!

So, let us now go over the essentials of the C++ code that you wrote that produced that simple on-screen output.

#include <iostream>

We call this symbol "#" as the hash symbol but in C++ programming we refer to them as *directives*. This part of the code gives instructions directly to the compiler program of your IDE. The keyword **"include"** after the directive tells the compiler to open and include a file (i.e. a certain file with pre-written codes in it so you don't have to type them anymore) with the code that you have written.
In this instance the file that is being accessed is the "iostream" file. This file is called a header file. There are other header files but we will begin with this one. The iostream file is necessary so that the input and output commands that you will write in your source code will work. It is placed at the top of a program because it is one of the first things (i.e. set of commands and functions that need to be included in your program source code) that should be performed.

using namespace std;

On line 2 of the source code that was provided, you will notice the keyword "**using**" – this part of the code tells the compiler that the code it is about to analyze and translate is using a library of commands. In this case the source code is using what is called the **standard library**. You'll see this line a lot of times when you write source codes in C++.

int main( )

This line indicates the start of the actual program that you are writing. It is called the **main( )** function. In other words, this is the main body of the program. Everything else that follows is only a subsection of the main program.
The open and close brackets "( )" indicate that the main body of the C++ program you are writing is actually a function. A function in the world of programming is a collection of different commands that is used to achieve a certain purpose or produce a certain output. In effect, all source codes that you will be writing are technically functions in programming terms.

Curly Brackets "{ }"

If you notice that after the main( ) function everything in the body of the program is inside the pair of curly brackets or curly braces found on lines 4 and 7 in the code above. All of the commands and programming statements that you will ever write in this program will be enclosed within these curly braces.

Notice also that all the lines of commands written in this code ends in a semicolon. To us human beings we end our sentences with a punctuation mark. In C++ programming there is only one punctuation mark and it only serves one purpose.

And that is to denote the end or terminus of a command. When a compiler reads that punctuation mark, it expects a new command to begin or the end of the program or some other part of the program to commence. If you forget that part of the syntax then the compiler will return an error and report it to you.

Now, don't worry about a lot about that for now. But when you have thousands of lines of code to work with, then that debugger part of the IDE will come in handy. Sometimes everything seems right when you look at things but minor details like a missing semicolon can cause an error that will take quite a while to locate if you edit your work manually.

cout << "Hello World!";

Line 5 in the sample code above is the "cout" statement. This statement tells the computer to output the characters that are enclosed within the double quotes. In this case it is the "Hello World!" line. Everything after the "<<" will be sent as a value of cout that will be outputted to the screen. Again the ";" semicolon at the end of this statement terminates the command.

return 0;

Line 6 in the sample program above has a return statement. This is statement that communicates to the operating system that is running on your device be it a computer, phone, or some other device.
In this case the statement "return 0;" is telling the operating system that everything went well when the program was executed and zero is returned and the program can be safely terminated.

Comments in C++

Remember how you can write little notes on the edges of a page when you're reading a book? The little scribbling doesn't affect the message of the author but it helps us the reader so we can have a better idea about what we are reading—I remember doing that when I was in college.
You can do that too in your source code. You can write little notes that will help you understand what's going on. The part of the source code that will be compiled won't be affected, just like what happens in a regular paperback or textbook.
So let's say we added a few notes on our source code. Add the following line to your code:

Run the program again through the compiler. Notice that even if you add the line "/* This part of the code is a comment */" it will have no effect on the output whatsoever.

Multiple Line Screen Output

Of course sometimes you want to format your output on several lines—let's say a list of stuff. To output to multiple lines, you can divide the string of characters using a "\n"— here's an example:

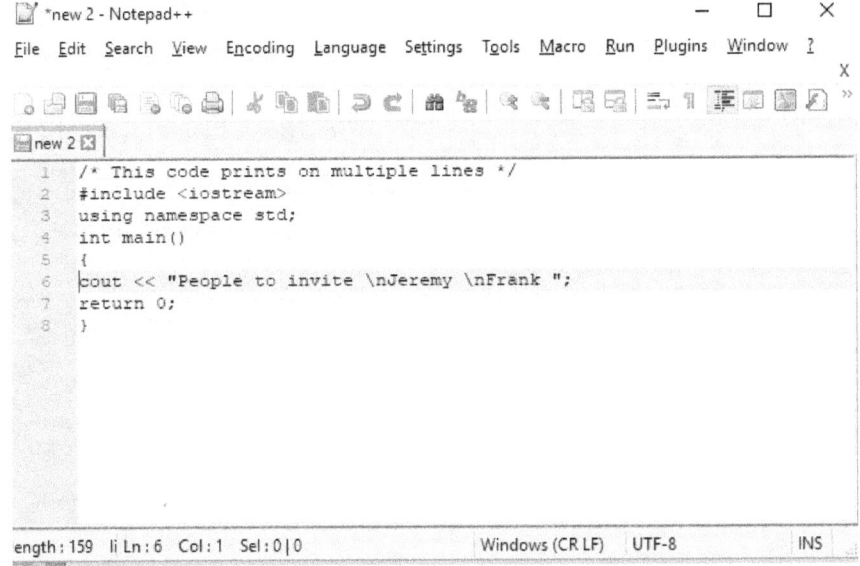

The output of that code will be as follows:

People to invite

Jeremy

Frank

Note that the "\n" doesn't get outputted to the screen. It means **newline**. It just tells the compiler to output the characters after it on the next line. The backslash "\" is called the **escape character**.
Here are other escape characters and their output on the screen:

\"	Outputs a double quote
\'	Outputs a single quote
\\	Outputs a backslash

\a	This is called a bell and it produces a beep sound
\t	Produces a horizontal tab
\n	This outputs the next characters into a new line

Chapter 3: Let's Do Some Math

One of the things that you will be doing a lot in programming is to do some math. In the source code example that we had in the previous chapter we only covered data that is static—they don't change. They just get outputted onto the screen and that's it.

Their values don't change. However, if you remember from good old algebra, there are mathematical constructs known as variables and they are represented by letters like a, b, c, x, y, and others

You also have variables in C++ but they aren't always represented by single letters. You can use single letters to represent variables and you can also use multiple characters (aka character strings).

What is a Variable?

A variable in C++ works very much like a variable in math (i.e. algebra). It is something that holds a value. It is called a "variable" simply because its value can change ergo its name. In programming and computer terms a variable is a way to access your computer's RAM (Random Access Memory), allocate a portion of that resource, and use it to store information or data.

The very first variable that we will introduce in this book is the "int" variable. There are other variable types of course but we will work with this one first. You can add that to your code this way for instance:

$$\text{int x;}$$

Okay so, we used "x" which is a common variable we solve for in math. You can declare several variables in sequence like this:

>int a;
>int x;
>int c

Of course that can seem tedious. That is why the code allows us to write all variables of the same type in this manner:

>int a, b, c;

You just have to separate each variable in your list using a comma. Now, we mentioned earlier that you can change the value of a variable. One way to do that is to assign a value to it. Here's an example:

>a = 50;
>b = 25;

Now, you can add those two variables together to change the value of the variable "c" declared above like this:

>c = a + b

To display the result you can use the "cout" command that you learned earlier. Gathering from what you have learned you might think of writing your code this way:

>cout << "Sum is equal to ";
>cout << c;

Notice that there are no quotation marks around the variable "c." You can actually combine both lines in C++ this way:

>cout << "Sum is equal to " << c;

Now, if you want a complete sample program that does all of that then here is a sample source code that does just that:

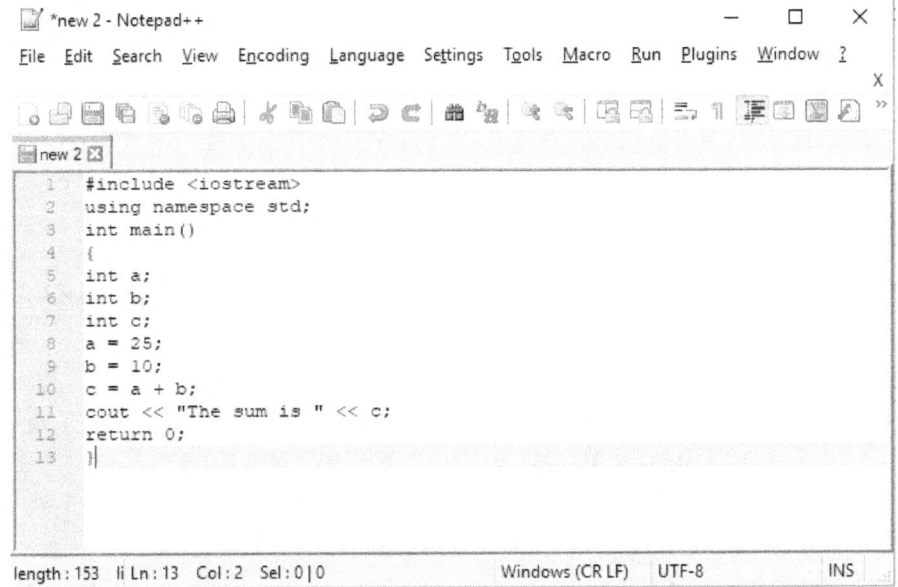

The output of this sample program will look like this:
The sum is 35

Get Creative with Your Identifiers

In the above example we used the letters a, b, and c as identifiers (i.e. the names we used) of 3 different variables. Identifiers can also be more than just single character names. We can actually replace the "c" identifier and use "sum" instead in our source code and it will work just fine.

As you can see the identifier "sum" is more descriptive and more human reader friendly compared to something as "c" which could mean anything. At least with a descriptive identifier, it can help you decipher what its purpose is in that source code.

This is important because one day someone else will edit your work in the not so distant future. Maybe they will review the program that you wrote and make necessary updates. Sure comments will work to help explain the details but using creative and descriptive names for your variable identifiers will make your source code a lot more readable and more human reader friendly.

However, in C++ there are several rules that you should follow when composing your variable identifiers. Here they are — your identifier name rules to live by:

- Your identifier can't be a reserve word (see next section in this chapter)
- You can use upper and/or lower case letters.
- Remember that C++ is case sensitive. That means the variables jEff and jeFF are two different things and will contain different values.
- Identifiers can't start with numbers
- An identifier can only contain letters, numbers, and underscores.

Reserved Words

As stated earlier, one of the rules when composing your identifier names is that you should not use reserved words. A reserved word is a word in C++ that is reserved for some other function. An example of that is "cout" which already means something is going to be displayed on the screen. Here are some of the most common reserved words (also known as keywords) in C++:

Asm
Auto

Bool
Break
case
catch
char
class
const
const_cast
continue
default
delete
do
double
dynamic_cast
else
enum
explicit
export
extern
false
float
for
friend
goto
if
inline
int
long
mutable
namespace
new
operator
private

protected
public
register
reinterpret_cast
return
short
signed
sizeof
static
static_cast
struct
switch
template
this
throw
true
try
typedef
typeid
typename
union
unsigned
using
virtual
void
volatile
wchar_t
while

So, what if you used one of these reserved words or keywords by mistake? If that is the case your compiler will be able to identify that error. You will be prompted about it so you can make the necessary correction.

Allowed Characters

The following are the characters that you are allowed to use when writing your C++ programs:

Letters of the Alphabet	a to z, A to Z
Whole numbers	0 to 9
Formatting	Space, backspace, carriage return, form feeds, and vertical and horizontal tabs
Special characters	^ \ + - * / () []$, ; : % {} = != <> ' "! & ? _ # <= >= @

Variables vs. Constants

As it was described earlier, a variable is a construct in C++ that changes its value. The opposite of that is a constant. A constant is similar to a variable (i.e. it contains a value) but its value does not change.

Here are the different types of constants in C++
- Decimal integers: any whole number (negative or positive) that does not begin with zero

- Octal integers: any whole number that starts with zero
- Hexadecimal integer: any integer that begins with ox or OX.
- Character constants: this is any character that is enclosed in single quotes (e.g. 'a', '10', '!' etc.)
- Floating constants: any real number (e.g. 3.1, -123.2, 5.0, -0.8)
- String literal: this is any series of characters enclosed in double quotes (e.g. "this Is a STRING 123.0 !")

Punctuators

Certain allowed special characters have a specific meaning in C++, which include the following:
- Parenthesis "( )" – also known as opening and closing brackets. They are used for grouping mathematical expressions and they are also used to signal the use of a function.
- Brackets "[ ]" – these are used for arrays (we'll go over that in a later chapter)
- Braces "{ }" – used to enclose groups of programming statements or commands.
- Comma "," – used to separate items in a list
- Semicolon ";" – terminates a statement

- Colon ":" – a conditional operator and it can also label a conditional statement
- Equal sign "=" – this is not used as a math operator. It is instead used to assign values to variables and other data structures.
- Asterisk "*" – math operator for multiplication. Also used in pointer declaration (more of that later).
- Hash sign "#" – used as directive for the preprocessor

Chapter 4: Let's Do More than Just Math

You have already been introduced to the concept of operators in C++ through the mathematical operator "+". There are actually other types of operators in this programming language other than the ones used for arithmetic. We'll go over the different types of operators in this chapter.

Types of Operators

Math Operators: The following are the arithmetic operators in C++
- \+ (addition)
- \- (subtraction)
- * (multiplication)
- / (division)
- % (modulus or remainder — only for integral data types)

Relational Operators: these are used to test the relationship between two values
- < (less than)
- \> (greater than)
- == (equal to)
- <= (less than or equal to)

- \>= (greater than or equal to)
- != (not equal to)

Logical Operators: you use these operators with relational operators to combine relational expressions.
- ! (not)
- && (and)
- || (or)

Unary Operators: these are used to tell whether a number is positive or negative. These require only one variable.
- -
- +

Assignment Operator: this is used to assign values to variables.
- =

Here are examples on how to use an assignment operator:
- a = 5 (the value assigned is 5)
- a = b = c = 12 (all variables a, b, and c take the value of 12)

Compound Assignments: for compound assignments (reduces length of code)
- +=
- -=
- %=

- /=
- *=

Example:
Let's say variable "a" has been assigned a value of 2. When you use it for a compound assignment like so:
$$a \mathrel{*}= 5$$
That is actually the equivalent of the expression a = a * 5 and the new value of "a" will be 10.

Increment and Decrement Operators
Incrementing means increasing the value by 1. A decrement is a decrease in value by 1. To increment a value use the ++ operator and to decrement use the - operator. You can place these operators before or after a variable.
Observe the following example:

```
int a, b;
int c = 5;
a = ++ c;
b = -- c;
```

After all the operations have been performed "a" will have a value of 6 while "b" will have a value of 4. That is a pre increment and a pre decrement. A post increment and post decrement will have a different effect:

```
int a, b;
int c = 5;
a = c ++;
b = c++;
```

After the operations have been done both "a" and "b" will have a value of 5 but "c" will have a new value of 6. In effect "a" and "b" take the original value of "c" before the increment and then c is incremented after the value assignment is completed.

Conditional Operator

A conditional operator tests whether an expression is true or false (yes, it is very much like math). And just like in math it will require three operands. The first operand is a conditional statement, and then it is followed by two expressions that need to be evaluated.
Here's an example:
$$\text{int a = 1, b = 2;}$$
$$c = (a > b) \text{ ? a : b;}$$
If the conditional expression in the example above is true then c takes on the value of a, but if it is false then c takes on the value of b. In this a > b is false that means c will take the value of b.

Sizeof Operator
Sometimes you need to know how much computer memory you need to store the value of a variable or a constant. I'm just putting this in here so you have some sort of reference but you won't do this that much in the beginning. This will become useful to you later when you tackle a bit more advanced C++ programming topics.
Here are a couple of examples:
$$\text{sizeof (float)}$$
$$\text{sizeof (char)}$$
The first siezeof in the example above will return a value of 1 while the second one will return a value of 4.

Operator Precedence

We know that in math there is precedence when we do arithmetic operations. If you have a series of math operations to perform, multiplication goes first followed by division, next by addition, and the last operation that you will perform is subtraction.

There is also an order of precedence in C++ and it is a bit longer than the one we have in math since we have a lot more operators in this programming language.

The following is the order of precedence in the operators in C++ from highest to lowest:

First	post ++ and --
Second	Pre ++ and -- sizeof ( ) !(not) -(unary) +(unary)
Third	* / % + -
Fourth	< <= > >= == !=
Fifth	&& ? :
Fifth	=

Programming Exercise

Write a program with three int variables x, y, and z. Initialize the value of x to 10 and y to 15. Increment the value of x then assign it to z. Add the value of x and y. Do a conditional operation checking if x is larger than y and store the value of either x or y to z. Output the value of z onto the screen.

Chapter 5: Data Types

You have already seen a few data types already. Now we will go through some more. C++ actually supports a lot of data types but we will only go over the basic ones here, which include the following:
- Integer
- Floating point numbers
- Characters
- Boolean

Fundamental Data Types

The following table lists the C++ fundamental data types with their descriptions.

Data Type	Description
int	Made up of integers or whole numbers. They include small integer numbers
long int	Includes all larger integers
float	Made up of real numbers or numbers that have a fractional part. This one only includes smaller real numbers.
double	This data type is for larger real numbers that can't be

	accommodated in small floating point.
long double	This is for long double precision numbers
char	This data type is refers to single characters

String Class

The string class is like the char variable type. The big difference is that it is composed of more than just one character. You can think of it as a bunch of characters strung together. C++ doesn't actually have a data type called string, what we have to work with instead is a string **class**.

We will go over classes in a later chapter of this book. For now just think of it as a way to store multiple characters in a variable.

```
#include <iostream>
#include <string> // Required in order to have a the string class in your program.
using namespace std;
int main ()
{
    string mystring = "This is an example of a string";
    cout << mystring;
    return 0;
}
```

Notice the additional #include directive on line 2. This is required so that you can use the string class in C++. After including that you can use the string class as you would any variable just like in line 6 in the example above.

Variable Initialization

To initialize a variable means to give it an initial value. Remember this acronym from programming: GIGO.
It stands for garbage-in garbage-out. One common beginner mistake is not to initialize your variables and use them straight in your source code. If you did not assign an initial value to a variable the compiler will use whatever random data is already stored in that part of the computer's RAM as the initial value of a variable. That of course will produce unwanted results.
In the examples that we have provided here, we have already shown you how to initialize your variables. For instance, line 6 of the string declaration sample code above is an initialization of a variable, which goes like this:
    string mystring = "This is an example of a string";
Other examples are:
        int x;
        x = 10;
        char gender;
        gender = f;

You use the assignment operator "=" to initialize variables. In the example above the first line "char gender" is the variable declaration. It is then followed by the variable initialization. Note that in C++ you need to declare a variable first before the compiler can use it in any operation. That is not the case in other programming languages though. You can actually declare your variable and initialize it in one line, like in this example:

char gender = f;

Another way to initialize variables is through a constructor (i.e. using a pair of parenthesis). Here is an example:

int x (1);

Take note that doing int x = 1; also produces the same effect. Yeah, it is kind of redundant but you will see the value of constructor initialization as you learn more advanced topics.

Type Conversions

Variables can be converted from one data type to another in C++. There are two types of this conversion that you should know about—implicit and explicit type conversions. When you work with numbers in reality you're not always going to compute using just whole numbers right?

You will be computing a mix of values like 5 multiplied 8.5 or10 divided by 1/2 or computing for the 5% of 350.2. So, how do you automate such computations in C++? Well, you do it via type implicit type conversions.

Here's an example how that is used in this programming language:

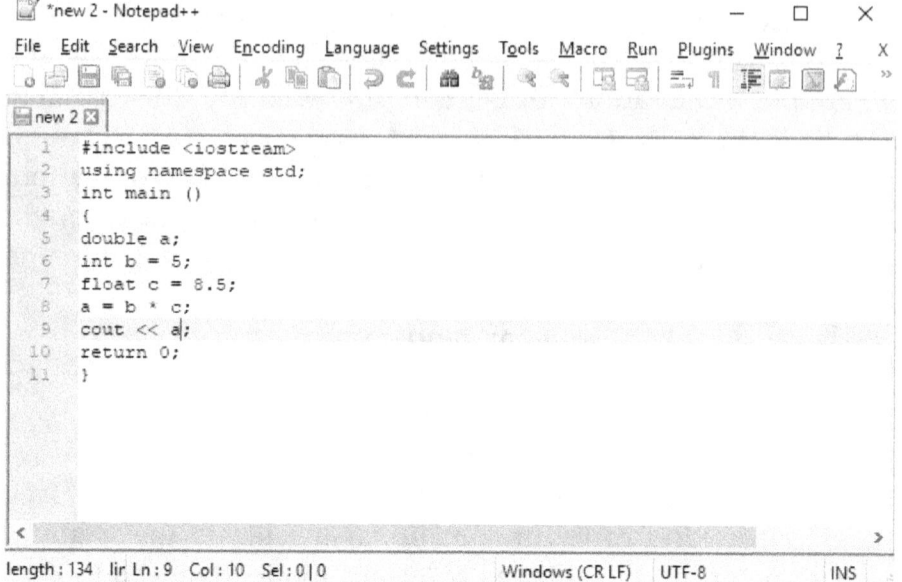

An explicit type conversion on the other hand is also called type casting and you will use the static_cast expression to perform such an operation. What it does is to convert the type of one variable temporarily before a computation is performed. Remember that this can only be done on the right hand side of an equation and not on the left.

For example we want to compute for the total commission that your sales team will get at the end of the month. You use a variable "total_sales" to compute for the total sales they made but this variable is a float type, which is what you needed at the time.

But then you needed to compute for a value total_commission, which has a larger range than what a float can give you. You will have to add the bonus for each sale, which inflates the amount. That means you need to temporarily convert total_sales from float to double before, and then add the bonus, and then save that value into total_commission (which is a double not a float).

To do just that use the following:

    total_commission = static_cast<double> (total_sales) + bonus;

Chapter 6: Input and Output

The input and output in C++ is handled by the standard library. Yes it is the iostream header file. What you have seen so far in our examples here are output to the screen using the cout object. You can actually output to other devices too such as a printer or a VDU.

You can also get input from the user of a computer asking them to enter certain values using a keyboard. You will use the "cin" statement to do that. Just remember that the cout object uses "<<" operator while the cin object uses ">>" operator.

Here are examples on how to use these two statements:
- cout << "Hi, my name is Frank!"; // prints a string
- cout << 250; // prints a numeric constant
- cout << salary; //prints the value of a variable
- cin >> area; // creates a cursor to the screen waiting for the user to enter a value

Here's another program that you can type and run using your C++ IDE. Type the following and execute it and observe how the cin and cout objects work. Remember that you can use the cout object to tell a computer user what to enter and the cin object can be used to receive input from the user. Now we are starting to make our C++ programs interactive with the use of the cin object.

```
// input output example
#include <iostream>
using namespace std;
int main ()
{
int length;
int breadth;
int area;
cout << "Please enter length of rectangle: ";
cin >> length;
cout << "Please enter breadth of rectangle: ";
cin >> breadth;
area = length * breadth;
cout << "Area of rectangle is " << area;
return 0;
}
```

Questions and Exercises:
1. Observe how the input is made using the cin object. Is the output using the cout object at the end correct?
2. Write another program this time computing for the area of a circle. You can assign the value of pi (i.e. 3.1416) to a float variable and use that to compute for the area. Make sure to ask a user to enter the radius of the circle being computed. Display the area of the circle at the end of program.

Using the cin Object to Enter Words

The cin object has limits. It cannot be used to allow computer users to enter entire sentences. If a user enters and entire sentence or several words, the cin object will only read up to the first space. That means it can only read one word at a time.

C++ resolves this issue by using the getline ( ) function. You will use it in tandem with the cin object. The getline function allows the cin object to continue reading word after word until it reaches the last word entered by a user.

Here is a sample source code that you can try. Observe the results.

```
1    // cin and strings
2    #include <iostream>
3    #include <string>
4    using namespace std;
5    int main ()
6    {
7    string name;
8    cout << "Enter your name";
9    getline (cin, name);
10   cout << "Hello " << name << "!\n";
11   return 0;
12   }
```

In this example, the user will be prompted to enter a name (which is a string value). Watch the syntax of the getline ( ) function. The arguments in that function include the cin object and the string variable separated by a comma. The output of course is the name of the person or the string that was entered.

In this example the user can enter his first and last name. Of course, you can enter more than just two words when using the getline ( ) function.

Chapter 7: Conditional Statements in C++

You have been introduced to conditional operators in chapters 3 and 4 of this book. This time we will go further into that by using conditional statements. You should know by now that a statement in C++ is a command that you give that the computer must perform.

Conditional Statements

A conditional statement tests a condition and will perform either of two operations depending on whether the condition is true or false. Here is a list of the conditional statements that you can use in this programming language:

If Statement
Here is the syntax of an if statement in C++

```
1   if (condition)
2   {
3       statement(s);
4   }
```

In **if statement**, the statements inside the { } will only be performed if the condition is true.

If Else Statement
The **if else statement** is like the **if statement** but it has two different statements. It will perform either of the two statements depending on whether the condition is true or not.

Here is an example:

```
1    if (x == 100)
2        cout << "x is 100";
3    else
4        cout << "x is not 100";
```

In the example above, if the value of the variable x is equal to 100 then the first cout statement in line 2 will be performed. If it is not then the second cout statement on line 4 will be performed.

Nested If Statements
You can place an **if statement** inside another **if statement** which gives you more options. This can be quite useful if you want to test for more than just one or two conditions. You can add more if statements as much as you need but you will have to closely or else you may be missing a detail or two and the compiler will prompt you that there is an error in your code.

Here is an easy example of a nested if statement.

```
1    if(percentage>=60)
2        cout<<"Ist division";
3    else if(percentage>=50)
4        cout<<"IInd division";
5    else if(percentage>=40)
6        cout<<"IIIrd division";
7    else
8        cout<<"Fail" ;
```

Notice that after each "else" it is followed by an if statement. Several conditions were tested and if any of the first 3 conditions were true then a certain line will be displayed on the screen. After any of these 4 possible outcomes are performed then the program will continue with the rest of the code.

Switch Statement

Notice that the if statement only allows for two branches in the decision. C++ allows you to create multiple branching options after checking a condition. Here is the syntax of a switch statement:

```
1    switch (var / expression)
2    {
3       case constant1 : statement 1;
4       break;
5       case constant2 : statement2;
6       break;
7       . .
8       default: statement3;
9       break;
10   }
```

The switch statement begins by evaluating the conditional expression. If the value of that expression is equal to the value contained in the variable then the statements that follow within the switch statement will be executed in sequence until one of the break statements is performed. If the value of a statement does not match any of the constants on that list then the default statement (in this example it's the one on line 8) is performed.

There is no specific order to the case values in this statement. The default on line 8 doesn't need to be at the end of the list. You can place it anywhere in the switch statement as needed. The expression within the switch statement (i.e. the one on line 1 in the example above) needs to be either a character or an integer.

Chapter 8: Loops

A loop in programming is an expression or command that is performed repeatedly. There are times when you have to repeat certain commands over and over until a specific condition has been reached. An example of that is to keep adding 5 to sum until you reach 100.

There are three types of loops that you can use in C++. They include the following:
- For loop
- While loop
- Do-while loop

For Loop

The For Loop is the easiest loop to make in C++. In this loop you already know in advance how many times a statement (or statements) should be repeated. That means you control and dictate how many loops or repetitions you have to make.

It has the following syntax:

```
for(initialization; condition ; increment/decrement)
{
    C++ statement(s);
}
```

Here is an example of a For Loop:

```
1   #include <iostream>
2   using namespace std;
3   int main(){
4       for(int i=1; i<=6; i++){
5           /* This statement would be executed
6            * repeatedly until the condition
7            * i<=6 returns false.
8            */
9           cout<<"Value of variable i is: "<<i<<endl;
10      }
11      return 0;
12  }
```

Focus on Efficiency

The output of that loop is to print the numbers 1 to 6 to the screen. Note that a lot of programmers prefer the For Loop over other loops in C++ but you should use whichever loop is best suited to perform a task. If a certain task will be more efficiently handled by other loops, then why force the use of a For Loop just because you prefer it over the others? Go for efficiency.

While Loop

In the While Loop a condition will be evaluated first. If it is true then the statements inside the loop will be performed. After that another evaluation will be made if the condition returns false then the loop ends.

Here is the syntax for this loop:

```
1   while(condition)
2   {
3       statement(s);
4   }
```

Here is an example of a While Loop:

```
1   #include <iostream>
2   using namespace std;
3   int main(){
4       int i=1;
5       /* The loop would continue to print
6        * the value of i until the given condition
7        * i<=6 returns false.
8        */
9       while(i<=6){
10          cout<<"Value of variable i is: "<<i<<endl; i++;
11      }
12  }
```

Do While Loop

In the While Loop statements will be performed repeatedly until the condition at the beginning will return false. The condition test is done first before any statements are performed. The Do While loop is almost the same except that the conditional testing is done after all the statements have been performed at least once. Remember: statements first, and then a conditional test after.

Here is the syntax for the Do While Loop in C++

```
1   do
2   {
3       statement(s);
4   } while(condition);
```

Here is a sample program you can try to run on your IDE that has a Do While loop:

```
1   #include <iostream>
2   using namespace std;
3   int main(){
4       int num=1;
5       do{
6           cout<<"Value of num: "<<num<<endl;
7           num++;
8       }while(num<=6);
9       return 0;
10  }
```

Jump Statements

Jump statements in C++ give you additional flow control. You don't want to be under the mercy of a loop while it is executing. One common programming mistake is an infinite loop where you construct your loop but it ends up continuously performing statements endlessly. It is more of a logical error than an actual bug in C++ – that means it is a problem with the programmer.

Jump statements help you transfer the control of the program flow inside a function. Essentially you make the program jump from one section of the code to the other, which can be helpful to break out of a loop if necessary. Think of it as a safeguard. Here are three jump statements that you need to learn as a beginner:

- Goto statement
- Break statement
- Continue statement

Go To Statement

A go to statement allows you to make the program jump from one part of the program to a designated section that you will label (i.e. that part of the program you will indicate). Here is the syntax of a go to statement:

goto label_name;

Here is the structure of this type of jump control statement:

```
1    label1:
2    ...
3    ...
4    goto label2;
5    ...
6    ..
7    label2:
8    ...
```

Note that you can place the go to statement anywhere in your C++ source code and you can make it jump to any label that you have created.

The following is an example of a source code that has a go to statement in it:

```
1   #include <iostream>
2   using namespace std;
3   int main(){
4       int num; cout<<"Enter a number: "; cin>>num;
5       if (num % 2==0){
6           goto print;
7       }
8       else {
9           cout<<"Odd Number";
10      }
11
12      print:
13      cout<<"Even Number";
14      return 0;
15  }
```

In this example the label is of the go to statement is "print" and this program is designed to evaluate and identify if the number entered by a user is an odd or even number. Notice that the go to statement makes the program jump out of the If Statement.

Break Statement

You can use a break statement to get out of a loop – in case something goes wrong during an operation of a loop that is. To break out of a loop you need to use an If Statement to terminate the loop that has gone wrong. That means you can only break a loop given certain conditions.

You can also use a break statement for a switch case control. That means the switch case has blocked (i.e. something went wrong). Best practice tells us that ever switch statement that you make should at least have a break statement inside it just in case. That way there is always a way for you to get out of the body of the switch statement in case something goes wrong.

Here is the syntax of the break statement:

break;

Let's go over a few examples of how a break statement is used. Our first example covers how to use a break statement to get out of a For Loop. The loop could have counted all the way to 200 but the break statement will make it stop at 197.

In our while loop example, we have a loop that will also execute or perform a count all the way to 200. But since there is a break statement that tests if the value of the variable is 12 then it makes the counting stop there.

In the example below with the switch statement we have breaks after each case block. If you remove those break statements every single statement within each case block will be executed or performed. As you can see below, a break statement provides more flow control within a switch statement.

Here is example number 1 with a for loop:

```cpp
#include <iostream>
using namespace std;
int main(){
    int var;
    for (var =200; var>=10; var --) {
        cout<<"var: "<<var<<endl;
        if (var==197) {
            break;
        }
    }
    cout<<"Hey, I'm out of the loop";
    return 0;
}
```

Here is example number 2 which has a break statement within a while loop:

```cpp
#include <iostream>
using namespace std;
int main(){
    int num =10;
    while(num<=200) {
        cout<<"Value of num is: "<<num<<endl;
        if (num==12) {
            break;
        }
        num++;
    }
    cout<<"Hey, I'm out of the loop";
    return 0;
}
```

This is example number three that has break statements within a switch statement:

```cpp
#include <iostream>
using namespace std;
int main(){
    int num=2;
    switch (num) {
        case 1: cout<<"Case 1 "<<endl;
        break;
        case 2: cout<<"Case 2 "<<endl;
        break;
        case 3: cout<<"Case 3 "<<endl;
        break;
        default: cout<<"Default "<<endl;
    }
    cout<<"Hey, I'm out of the switch case";
    return 0;
}
```

Programming Exercise

Write a program that has a d0-while statement in it. Make the program count from 1 to 10 and then display the numbers on screen. Rewrite the C++ program to include a break statement within the do while loop. Make the loop break when the count reaches 5.

Continue Statement

A continue statement is also used inside loops in C++ just like a break statement. The difference here is that a break statement makes the program flow jump outside of the loop while a continue statement merely jump starts the loop to go back to the beginning and start all over again. That is when the loop goes to a continue statement all the other statements after the continue statement gets ignored and the loop goes back to start.

Here is the syntax of a continue statement:

continue;

The following is an example of a For Loop that has a continue statement in it. This program will display the numbers 1 to 5. However, the loop has a continue statement inside it that checks if the value of the variable "num" is equal to three. In effect, the loop will print to the screen the numbers 1 to 5 except for the number 3. Try this source code—type it in your IDE and run it.

```
#include <iostream>
using namespace std;
int main() {
    for (int num=0; num<=6; num++) {
        /* This means that when the value of
         * num is equal to 3 this continue statement
         * would be encountered, which would make the
         * control to jump to the beginning of loop for
         * next iteration, skipping the current iteration
         */

        if (num==3) {
            continue;
        }
        cout<<num<<" ";
    }
    return 0;
}
```

Chapter 9: C++ Functions

We have mentioned functions in an earlier chapter of this book. In fact you have already used them in some of the sample programs as well as in the exercises too. In fact, you already know the main ( ) function. You've been using it all this time. We'll cover what functions are in this chapter and how you can use them.

What is a Function?

A function in C++ is actually a block of code or a group of statements and other pieces of code that have been packaged together. This code performs a specific function or task, which is why they are collectively called a function in C++ programming. There are functions already built into C++ but you can always make your own. That way you can create ones that can solve or do a specific task that you need at certain parts of a program.

The following is the syntax for a function in C++

```
1   return_type function_name (parameter_list)
2   {
3       //C++ Statements
4   }
```

Here is an example of a source code that contains a function in this programming language:

```
1   #include <iostream>
2   using namespace std;
3   /* This function adds two integer values
4    * and returns the result
5    */int
6   sum(int num1, int num2){
7       int num3 = num1+num2; return num3;
8   }
9
10  int main(){
11      //Calling the function
12      cout<<sum(1,99);
13      return 0;
14  }
```

Function Declarations

You can declare functions in C++ before or after the main ( ) function. Just remember that if you define the function at the beginning of the program source code (i.e. before the main () function) then then you don't need to do a function declaration.

However, you can also do a function declaration after the main () function. If that is the case then you should do your function declaration first and then you can use the function within the rest of the code. If you do not do that then the compiler will return an error.

Here is the syntax of a function declaration in C++

    return_type function_name(parameter_list);
      { //statements inside the function}

Remember that when making your function declarations you can skip adding the parameter names (the ones inside the parameter_list). You can make your declarations like this:

      int total(int,int);

Instead of:

      int total(int num1,int num2);

Note that you can do it according to the short form above and you won't encounter any problems.

To call or use a function all you need to do is to add to a statement in your source code complete with the necessary parameters.

Here is a sample source code that has a function in it with a function declaration. Pay attention to where the function was declared and how it was used inside the body of the source code.

```
1   #include <iostream>
2   using namespace std;
3   //Function declaration
4   int sum(int,int);
5
6   //Main function
7   int main(){
8       //Calling the function
9       cout<<sum(1,99);
10      return 0;
11  }
12  /* Function is defined after the main method
13   */
14  int sum(int num1, int num2){
15      int num3 = num1+num2;
16      return num3;
17  }
```

Built-In Functions

We have already mentioned that there are two types of functions—some are already built into C++ and they are called built-in functions. The other type of functions in this programming language is called the user defined functions. These are the functions that we write ourselves just like the ones in the examples above.

You don't need to declare built-in functions since they are already part of the entire system. Your compiler will just add the code for a built-in function any time you call it within the body of your program when the source code gets compiled or translated.

The following is an example of a source code that you can try that makes use of the built-in function pow( ):

```
1   #include <iostream>
2   #include <cmath>
3   using namespace std;
4   int main(){
5       /* Calling the built-in function
6        * pow(x, y) which is x to the power y
7        * We are directly calling this function
8        */
9       cout<<pow(2,5);
10      return 0;
11  }
```

Here is a list of built in functions in C++. Note that some of them are math functions while the others are character functions.

| sqrt(x) | Gives you the square root of |

		x
pow(x, y)		Gives you the value of x raised by the exponent which is the value of y
sin(x)		Produces the sine of the angle expressed by x. The measurement returned will be in radians.
cos(x)		Gives you the cosine of the angle denoted by x and it is going to be measured in radians
tan(x)		This function gives you the tangent of the angle expressed by x and its measurement will outputted in the number of raidans
abs(x)		This function will return the absolute value of the number in its argument in integers
isalpha(c)		Returns true if the argument c is a capital letter, returns false if it is in small caps
isdigit(c)		Returns true or false depending if the argument c is a number from 0 to 9
isalnum(c)		This function returns true if argument c is either a number or a character
isupper(c)		This function returns true if argument c is an uppercase letter.

islower(c)	This function returns true if argument c is lowercase
toupper(c)	It converts argument c to uppercase
tolower(c)	This function converts argument c to lower case

Chapter 10: Arrays

All of the variables that we have seen so far through the examples and sample source code that we have provided thus far contain single values. On top of that every variable that we have created only contains one type of data. Sometimes it is just an integer, a floating point number, or a character.

However, variables don't have to be that way. There are variables in C++ that can contain more than one value. Yes, there are constructs in this programming language that can contain a lot of values. They are more complex records than what we have learned so far.

On top of that there are constructs in C++ programming that can contain more than one value and those values are of different types of data. That means one may contain a mix of numbers, characters, and strings. We'll go over that in a separate section of this book.

What is an Array?

An array is a data structure in C++ programming that is more complex than the variables that we have already introduced here. You are now moving your programming knowledge up a notch learning this concept.

Technically speaking, an array is a variable that contains several items or values of the same type. In programming terms, there are times when just one variable isn't enough to hold the data that is needed or required. An array may be able to help you with that.

For example, you may want to record the scores of 100 different students after an exam. It will be a bit too tedious if have to declare and use 100 different variables inside your program.

Not only that, you will also have to deal with names of each variable. Each one should match and represent each student that took the exam. If you follow this programming strategy, you won't be able to use this same program next year since you will have a different set of students and obviously they will also have totally different names.

In this case a single array that can contain all the scores will be very useful. You can store, access, and modify the scores as needed and all you need is just one data structure. It simplifies everything and makes everything easier to track.

Array Declaration

There are two ways that you can use to define or declare an array in your C++ source code. Here is the first way that you can do that:

```
1   int arr[5];
2   arr[0] = 10;
3   arr[1] = 20;
4   arr[2] = 30;
5   arr[3] = 40;
6   arr[4] = 50;
```

In this method arr[0] to arr[4] represent the memory allocations that have been grouped into one variable called "arr". In the declaration above (i.e. line 1), the variable "arr" is an int type and it has a total of 5 compartments.

To access the values stored in the array you need to indicate the name of the variable + the compartment (this is called the index). So the formula is arr + index. The index starts with 0 and the last index is the number declared minus 1.

So, in case you want to access the last index in the variable arr, you need to use arr[4] and not arr[5]. In the example above arr[4] which is the 5th in the series of indices, contains the value of 50.

Here is the second way you can declare an array in C++

```
1    int arr[] = {10, 20, 30, 40, 50};
```

Notice that this is a simpler way to declare your array and assign values to each of the indices. Note however, that the compiler will determine the value in arr[ ] depending on the number of values that you use to initialize your array. This way you can keep initializing your array without having to worry about the number of indices you already have.

And there is a third way to declare an array in this programming language, which you will see below:

```
1    int arr[5] = {10, 20, 30, 40, 50};
```

In this third method you also shorten the array declaration but you indicate the number of indices that you will use.

Accessing Array Data

You can access the elements in an array by using the index number. Remember that it starts with 0 and ends with the last number in the indicated index declaration minus 1. Here's another example that you can try which illustrates this principle:

```
1   #include <iostream>
2   using namespace std;
3
4   int main(){
5       int arr[] = {11, 22, 33, 44, 55};
6       cout<<arr[0]<<endl;
7       cout<<arr[1]<<endl;
8       cout<<arr[2]<<endl;
9       cout<<arr[3]<<endl;
10      cout<<arr[4]<<endl;
11      return 0;
12  }
```

The output of the sample program above is the series of numbers 11, 22, 33, 44, and 55 outputted on screen in different lines. As you can see, accessing and displaying the contents of the indices of the array is rather tedious since you will have to repetitively.

You guessed it right if you think you can use a loop to access and display the values stored in an array. Here is the same program with a little tweak to it. This variation uses a loop to display the contents of the array. It is the preferred method amongst C++ programmers and it is also more efficient.

```
1   #include <iostream>
2   using namespace std;
3
4   int main(){
5       int arr[] = {11, 22, 33, 44, 55};
6       int n=0;
7
8       while(n<=4){
9           cout<<arr[n]<<endl;
10          n++;
11      }
12      return 0;
13  }
```

Multidimensional Arrays

Now, what we have seen so far is an array that is one dimensional. That means it only contains one series of values. Again, arrays and other data structures in programming can be more complex than that so that they can handle more difficult tasks and solve more complex problems.

Moving your array knowledge up a notch we will now cover two dimensional arrays. The single dimensional arrays that we have gone over so far will look like a table with only one row, like this:

| 11 | 22 | 33 | 44 | 55 |

That is taking the values from our latest example earlier. Now, a 2 dimensional array will be something like that but it will contain more rows. This makes the information or data stored inside your array to be more tabular. So, let's say we want to store more values in it, then we can make a multi-dimensional array and its data and indices will look like this:

11	22	33	44	55
66	77	88	99	12
13	14	15	56	67
78	89	90	23	34

Now your array has 5 columns and 4 rows. That makes your array a more powerful tool when it comes to programming in C++. Here's how you can declare a two dimensional array:

$$int\ arr[2][3];$$

In this sample declaration you will have a total of 6 elements in your array, which is derived from 2 * 3 for a total of 6. You can imagine that as 2 rows and 6 columns.

You can also create a three dimensional array. This is a more complex kind of array and unfortunately it can't be represented in tabular terms since it is in 3D.

Here is a sample declaration:

int arr[3][3][3];

In this sample declaration you will have 3 * 3 * 3 number of elements in one array, which gives you a total of 27 elements inside your array.

The next question is how you can initialize the values of the different array elements. Well, you can use the same initialization methods described above. You can initialize them using direct reference calling each element one by one, which is rather tedious. Another way of course is by using a loop, which would shorten your code. Let's say you have a 2 dimensional array and you want to initialize it manually. Here are two ways you can do just that.

The first sample method would be the following:

int arr[2][2] = {10, 11 ,12 ,20};

Notice that this method doesn't help you visualize the rows and columns of the array. If you want a more visual kind of declaration, then do the following:

int arr[2][2] = { {10, 11} , {12 ,20} };

In the second method, you can imagine the values 10 and 11 as the top row and then 12 and 20 as the second row.

Programming Exercise

Write a program that contains a two dimensional array which has a 3 x 3 matrix (i.e. [3] [3]). Initialize the values or elements using a loop.

Accessing Multi-Dimensional Array Elements

You access multi-dimensional arrays the same way you would a single dimensional array. You always begin with [0][0] for the first element first row. To access the second element first row use [0][1] and so on for the other elements in the series.

Now, if you want to access the second row first element use [1][0], [1][1] for second row second element, and so forth.

If you want to access the third row first element use [2][0], and then [2][1] for the second, [2][2] for the third and so forth for every element in that row.

Here is a sample source code that uses a two dimensional array:

```
1  #include <iostream>
2  using namespace std;
3
4  int main(){
5      int arr[2][3] = {{11, 22, 33}, {44, 55, 66}};
6      for(int i=0; i<2;i++){
7          for(int j=0; j<3; j++){
8              cout<<"arr["<<i<<"]["<<j<<"]: "<<arr[i][j]<<end
9          }
10     }
11     return 0;
12 }
```

In this example we have a program in C++ that uses a three dimensional array:

```cpp
#include <iostream>
using namespace std;

int main(){
    // initializing the array
    int arr[2][3][2] = {
        { {1,-1}, {2,-2}, {3,-3} },
        { {4,-4}, {5,-5}, {6,-6} }
    };
    // displaying array values
    for (int x = 0; x < 2; x++) {
        for (int y = 0; y < 3; y++) {
            for (int z = 0; z < 2; z++) {
                cout<<arr[x][y][z]<<" ";
            }
        }
    }
    return 0;
}
```

Programming Challenge

Here is a programming challenge that I would like you to try and solve. This will be a combination of all the programming principles that you have learned so far. Take your time and try to write the program according to the instructions below.

1. Create 3 arrays that are multidimensional (2 dimensions each). Do not indicate the number of elements for each argument.

2. Create a dialogue for the computer user asking him/her to enter the number of rows and columns of the arrays.
3. Ask the user to enter each of the elements for the two arrays. Enter the values in each of the elements of the two arrays.
4. Add the values of the elements of the two matrices.
5. Store the added values from the 2 matrices/arrays to the 3rd array.
6. Display the contents of all the elements of the 3rd array onto the screen.

Now, this exercise will be a big test. But the good news is that we have the answers on the next page. Please write the program as best as you can. Pay attention to the errors that your IDE will give you in case you do encounter errors.

The answer is on the next page.

Answer to Programming Challenge

Here is my version of the correct program that answers the challenge in the previous page:

```cpp
#include<iostream>
using namespace std;

int main()
{
    int row, col, m1[10][10], m2[10][10], sum[10][10];

    cout<<"Enter the number of rows(should be >1 and <10): ";
    cin>>row;
    cout<<"Enter the number of column(should be >1 and <10): ";
    cin>>col;
    cout << "Enter the elements of first 1st matrix: ";
    for (int i = 0;i<row;i++ ) {
      for (int j = 0;j < col;j++ ) {
         cin>>m1[i][j];
      }
    }
    cout << "Enter the elements of first 1st matrix: ";
    for (int i = 0;i<row;i++ ) {
      for (int j = 0;j<col;j++ ) {
         cin>>m2[i][j];
      }
    }

    cout<<"Output: ";
    for (int i = 0;i<row;i++ ) {
      for (int j = 0;j<col;j++ ) {
         sum[i][j]=m1[i][j]+m2[i][j];
         cout<<sum[i][j]<<" ";
      }
    }

    return 0;
}
```

Chapter 11: Pointers

When you learn pointers you begin to delve into dynamic data in the world of programming. All of the variables that we have seen so far are static. Once you declare them – then that's it. Pointers are different in that they are dynamic. You can create more of them as the program keeps on running and interacting with users and other program elements.

What is a Pointer?

A pointer is also a variable in C++. However, you can call it as an advanced type of variable. Apart from what has already been explained, another important feature that makes a pointer unique is the fact that it doesn't contain any data or actual value that a user or program function can directly use.

What pointers contain is the memory address where you can find the data that you will need. This is a very important kind of concept that you should learn. Certain advanced programming constructs such as linked lists rely on this theory.

Declaring a Pointer

The following is the syntax for pointers:
                data_type *pointer_name;
Now, here is a sample pointer declaration:

```
1    /* This pointer p can hold the address of an integer
2     * variable, here p is a pointer and var is just a
3     * simple integer variable
4     */
5    int *p, var
```

When declaring a pointer you begin with the type of data you want the pointer to point to, the name of the pointer variable preceded by an asterisk, and then followed by a variable.

You don't always have to put a variable at the end. You can also just end the declaration with the pointer name preceded by the asterisk, like this:
                int * pNumberOne;

TIP: Now, here's a naming convention among programmers. Do you notice the small letter "p" in pNumberOne? It's not required but many programmers use that style of naming to denote that pNumberOne or some other variable name is a pointer and not just some other variable in the program.

Making Use of Pointers

In order to make use of pointers you need to have it point to something. In order to do that, you will need to use the ampersand symbol "&". That is how you assign the address of a variable to your pointer.

If we use our first example we will use the following line to make that assignment:

$$p = \&var;$$

If we want to use our second example, we would do it this way:

$$pNumberOne = \&var$$

At this point we have both p and pNumberOne pointing to the int variable named var. We can then do two things:
- Access the memory address of the variable var
- Access the value stored in var through the use of pointers (which is an indirect way of accessing that data.

Let's say we want to output the memory address of var to the screen using the pointers we made, we can use the following statements:

$$cout << p;$$
$$cout << pNumberOne;$$

Both statements produce the same output, which is the memory address of var. But what if we want to access the value stored in var? Here's how you can do that:

$$cout << *p;$$
$$cout << *pNumberOne;$$

From what we have learned so far the ampersand sign "&" denotes the memory address of the variable being pointed to. By adding an asterisk to the pointer it dereferences it, which means you are instead accessing the value of the variable being pointed to.

Here's a sample program that you can run and analyze to help you understand how pointers work as well as how you can use them.

```cpp
1   #include <iostream>
2   using namespace std;
3   int main(){
4       //Pointer declaration
5       int *p, var=101;
6
7       //Assignment
8       p = &var;
9
10      cout<<"Address of var: "<<&var<<endl;
11      cout<<"Address of var: "<<p<<endl;
12      cout<<"Address of p: "<<&p<<endl;
13      cout<<"Value of var: "<<*p;
14      return 0;
15  }
```

Now, this is a lot to take in and it can be outright confusing for beginners. I advise that you read over all of that at least twice. You won't see the value of knowing the memory address of a variable at first. And at this time you may be wondering why in the world you would want to access the value of a variable indirectly through a pointer.

This is a bit of an advanced topic but I'm just laying it out here so you can have a basic understanding of pointers. You will learn more of that as you master C++ programming.

Moving Forward

You have now gone over the most basic and fundamental principles behind C++ programming. What you have learned so far is to create programs that are procedural in nature. This type of programming approach is very easy to grasp because that is usually how we approach tasks.

We think of them as steps that we need to go over one by one until a problem is solved. There is actually another approach that you will need to learn, which will eventually make things easier to do tasks and resolve problems. And that is called object oriented programming or OOP for short.

What is OOP?

The objective in OOP is to break down a complex issue, task, or problem into smaller doable tasks/problems. To do that we use what is called an object. We have already mentioned a few objects in this book and in fact we have used them a little bit.

Objects are programming constructs that can interact with one another. They're not just stand alone set of instructions that need to be done. These objects work with one another to perform a task or solve a problem.

OOP also uses classes, polymorphism, inheritances, encapsulation, and data abstraction. Again, this is a lot to take in and it will be made a lot easier after an expansion of this book. But we'll just go over the basic concepts at this point.

Classes vs. Objects

In OOP you will primarily use objects and classes. A class in C++ OOP is a blueprint. Think of it as a model or mold that you can use to create something—well you use it to create the object to be exact. It isn't the object itself since a class is nothing more than a model or a mold (i.e. a blueprint).
With that single class (or blueprint or mold) you can create as many objects as you need so as to solve a problem. So let's say the problem is assigning school buses to take students to school. The problem is we need a way to assign multiple buses to different numbers of students in a huge campus.
Instead of writing a finite number of buses—something that isn't feasible in the long run coz buses can break down and replaced eventually. So you use classes to make your computer records of these buses to be dynamic. You can create and delete the actual buses created using the class which we will call sChoolBus.
To create that class, simply use the following line:
                    class sChoolBus;

There is no naming convention here. I just wanted to make the name of that class as memorable to you as possible. Now, here's something cool about classes and objects. Your class and objects can contain different types of data all mixed inside it.

It's like an array but arrays only contain data of the type, remember? You can make it as multi-dimension as you want to but at the end of the day if it is an int type then all it will ever contain are integers.

Classes and the objects that you create can contain different types of variables and data. So, let's say a sChoolBus class should contain the bus number, the number of students that can ride in it, the name of the driver, and the time it is supposed to arrive in school. Here's a sample declaration for that class:

```
1   class sChoolBus
2   {
3       //Data members
4       char name_ofdriver[20];
5       int capacity;
6       int bus_number;
7       float time_schedule;
8   };
```

Now, if you want to create an object under the sChoolBus class simply do the following:

```
class universitybus1;
```

You now have an object in your program called universitybus1 that can store the records of that school bus. If your school happens to acquire more school buses then you just need to create more records. As the information for these buses change, you can make changes directly to these records.

Again, this will also sound a lot to take in especially for someone who has no prior programming knowledge. At least now you see the potential for this type of programming approach and C++ is a great way to get to it.

A Final Word

I hope that the lessons and exercises that you have worked through here in this book has helped you understand the most fundamental programming concepts. You can always go back to the previous lessons to help you recall how each of these concepts fit in with the rest.
I hope that the information here has inspired you to enjoy programming and coding in C++ and has encouraged you to keep on learning.
To your success!
Thank you again for downloading this book.

www.ingramcontent.com/pod-product-compliance
Lightning Source LLC
Chambersburg PA
CBHW072201170526
45158CB00004BB/1725